American Family:
A Syndrome

poems by

Nandi Comer

Finishing Line Press
Georgetown, Kentucky

American Family:
A Syndrome

ACKNOWLEDGMENTS

Thank you to the following editors and staff of the journals and anthologies
in which these poems originally appeared:

Blue Shift Journal: "Singing Skin Disorder"
Callaloo: "Ostrich Woman"
Cave Canem Anthology XII: Poems 2008-2010: "Assembling Mother"
The New Sound: "Car Slams into House, Lands on Sleeping Man;" "Your Eyes
Have Never Looked This Stunning"
The Offing: "Ode to Sofia's Mouth"
Pluck! Journal of Affrilation Arts & Culture: "Why I Don't Call on Cops"
Third Coast: "Chicken"
www.backroomlive.wordpress.com: "Assembling Mother"

Publisher: Leah Maines
Editor: Christen Kincaid
Cover Art: Sydney James
Author Photo: Nandi Comer
Cover Design: Elizabeth Maines McCleavy

Printed in the USA on acid-free paper.
Order online: www.finishinglinepress.com
             also available on amazon.com

Author inquiries and mail orders:
Finishing Line Press
P. O. Box 1626
Georgetown, Kentucky 40324
U. S. A.

Table of Contents

for my mother, Kafi Tene (July 1952 – July 2016)
and
my father, Gregory McAfee (October 1953 – February 2017)

Dear Reader,

This is a private conversation.
Americana circa all the centuries:
Boy Lynched at Daylight
on city canvas, or southern
back road, or blog.
Dear Trayvon, look
what you started. Torso reclined
on pale boulder, head tucked
under right elbow. Left hand still
in coat pocket.
Dear Reader, please,
do not read further.
Dear Michael,
I try to ignore
your face and peace sign and
your mother crying next to
Trayvon's mother next to Sean's mother
next to Emitt's ghost.
Dear woman in another city
pleading, I am ready to mourn you.
Death designs my face. Dear reader,
I am not talking to you.
Dear cell phone, please stay
in your pockets, your purse.
Do not record. Do not post.
If there is blood, the artist
chose to omit it. Dear sheriff.
Dear sergeant. Dear
security guard. And the boy
remains transfixed in his last
breath. Dear principal. Dear counselor.
Dear parent. Dear man
I am passing, my name is—
Dear internet, please
do not post my slaughter.

Dear every man I know, stop.
Don't move. Don't
put your hands up. Do not stop.
Remain. Dear unnamed black man
killed again, and again and again.
Dear___, are you surprised?
Dear reader, no.

American Family: A Syndrome
Early Death Syndrome (EDS)

Remember that time cops
found cousin Rosa
on the East Side
carjacking some woman?

Said she stepped right in front
of a silver Caprice,
pulled that frightened lady
out of her car,
like a rag. Remember

how her daughter had to go
down to the precinct,
had to explain that
her mother got them voices?
Remember her brother—

that slim shell of a boy—
how he put three bullets
in their mother,
then left himself shot
and dead in the drive?

Coward
Uncle Otha called him.
The *Devil* said mama.
hypoparanoidschizophrenic
say the docs.

And remember
that girl he loved?
When she heard
she dropped all her body,
rubber band legs
and horse shoulders,

Terminal Illness—Upon
learning the short life
expectancy of men and women
from his/her community, a
patient suffering from EDS
embraces the inevitability
of an early death. Usual
signs of EDS exhibit in black
males and females ranging
from ages 10 to 35. Early
symptoms include testing
the limitations of pain by
engaging in suicidal activities
such as dislocating joints out
of sockets, jumping from
rooftops and/or participating
in backyard mixed martial
arts competitions. Generally
these activities are followed by
an unhealthy consumption of
processed food and insomnia.

In many cases a patient
imagines his limbs
disappearing and reappearing.
Most patients have been
known to whisper to friends
and family that they are
already gone. Almost all have
experienced dreams depicting
their own deaths and/or
funerals. Patients express
debilitating survival behavior
such as, a distrust all strangers
and feelings of constant
endangerment. At the same
time the knowledge of an
early demise causes fearless
behavior.

dropped them all
in the middle of the den,
like a sack of oranges.
Remember

how the whole family
came to the cemetery
to put mother and son
in the ground;
how Rosa refused
to buy the coffins?
Said she'd rather
build boxes
from the planks
of her picket fence;
said each board
carried the sound
of her family's
southern snared grief,
each of her dead
meshed with the wood grain.
And who hasn't seen Death—

that ruthless engineer—
stack the bricks
of this rickety house,
one broken brain
on top of another.
Rosa's uncle took his wife by knife
and cousin Robert still hold
a bullet in his back
from when his mother
tried and failed.
Death can be relentless
with his building, cain't he?
You remember Rosa in the street

Some have been known to stand in close proximity to high-speed traffic, while others resort to consuming poisonous substances. In most common cases, patients violently provoke others suffering from the same illness. In rare occurrences patients develop debilitating behavior similar to the avoidant personality disorder otherwise known as the Hermit Complex.

Unfortunately, neither denying nor provoking an early death has proven to be resourceful in the treatment of this fatal disease.

Almost all patients find their demise under the following circumstance: violence inflicted by a member of private security, mistaken identity by law enforcement, self-inflicted wounds or lethal assault by private citizens.

screaming down at that woman?
Something about the car
or was it something about her brother—
I mean granddad
or was it about auntie
or me
or—

Inevitably in its final stages of taking over the body, all patients suffering from this illness utter the following statements moments before passing: *I can't breathe. Why are you treating me like this? I didn't do anything wrong. What did I do? Please stop. You are hurting me.*

Assembling Mother

Teeth from the riverbank,
a knee from the playground,
we always find the ears
first. Brother finds her arms
in the sink again. We bring
all of her in pails to her bedroom.
We refasten every heavy part.
Sometimes brother can't find
all of her so we give her
someone's hands. She sobs
when she gets her eyes,
begins twisting around the house,
limps out the front door.
We grab our gathering buckets.

On Coming Home To Teach

I tell my student he is not a corpse. *I know.*
I am a wrecked train. I show him

my scars. He holds up a hand, peeks
through a hole some boys stabbed

out of his palm. We've never seen each other
outside school, but we wake

on the same block to a woman
damning a man's fists.

He sneaks into gated backyards
where chained pit bulls lurch.

Hope is the snap of their angry collars.
I've known what it is to pacify panic.

Singing words are useless, cold water
splashed over sidewalk blood. When I leave

he will cut off his tongue, tame his outbursts.
Each day Death will bend his body into his desk.

If I speak for him, it will only return my fear.
If I speak for him, this poem is his suicide note.

American Family: A Syndrome
Singing Skin Disorder

It's the humming—not notes.
Not a melody. It's a signal. A rattle

nesting in my joints.

Like the snarl of yard mutts,
the clipped chirp

of an unhinged ceiling fan.

When they sit near me
some brown, soupy ditty

scurries down my spine.

Like they've trapped a rusty
robin in their elbows.

Modulated and molded.

Pored. Pock-marked. Smooth
as an infant's innocence.

Skin.

There's this thing I see every morning
on the AM bus.

Who sees twelve-year old legs?

A book bag? A girl?
It says "Come."

It sings, "I am your now."

Inconclusive Disorder—
Patients under observation
have displayed symptoms of
Singing Skin Disorder (SSD)
where patients' pores emit a
melody-like auditory sound,
much like that of a bird or
whale call. Patients with darker
pigmentation appear to have
larger pores, and often times
their skin emits an offensive,
less melodic tonal pitch than
those with less melanin.

Under microscopic evaluation
of skin samples, there seems to
be no distinguishable markers
in any of the documented SSD
patients that differentiate them
from non-SSD patients.

All of the doctors in our
observation facilities have
heard the songs. Patients
under observation report
hearing skin songs of other
patients, however all evidence
point to a lack of auditory
recognition of their own,
leaving us to believe this is a
type of auditory pheromone
or territorial marking made
by the body wherein the host
is unaware.

This high pitched lilt
chucks its volume down the street.

Its trickster, blow-pop smile is a mistake,

is anger, a wily, guttural ruse. Deep
under her skin, her hollow jingle jabs my ribs

makes me want to slam a face to the ground

Such danger in those open hands.
Can't you hear the quiet composition?

The falsetto pitch and thrust?

Oh, to have that song
running running running through me.

On occasion we have tried to record the music of SSD patients, but upon playback, the recordings contain no sound. Along with no evidence of patients hearing their own skin, the lack of documentation leaves doubt as to if the songs actually exist.

Whether SSD is temporary, permanent or actual is inconclusive.

On Placing My Mother on a Ceramic Oval
after Solmaz Sharif

my mother tipping her cane   my mother
struggling with buttons   her slow unsteady pace

my mother leaning into the kitchen sink
my mother sucking down cake   sucking down

a candy   down some forbidden sweet   my father
telling his wife he will not come home tonight again

because he is working on women who are not mothers
my brother upstairs silent   my mother slamming

cabinet doors   banging the bathroom door   slams jars
into shards and blames us for the constellation of glass

my mother alone   always humming another tone deaf tune
my mother's sister insists and insists on visiting

location   a place I am now obliged to visit   are we supposed
to talk   my mother's sister passes cash under my chin

this is for you and your brother says my father
and I am happy I do not have a child   I will not be visited

brought back   called back by my living   and she passes
cash under my nose   my mother is losing

her bowels   my mother greets all strangers with her
polite voice she retains for strangers   my mother so silent

my aunt slides the cash across the room
my mother is still breathing my father insists   my aunt insists

on visiting a ceramic oval of a picture I already own.

Anarcha Appears Again and Again
after Rachel Eliza Griffiths

Once I was slave, then I was an Alabama woman,
a hushed experiment hidden between the damp thighs

of Tuskegee men. Too many times I was a newborn
next to my mother in LA General County Hospital,

her slick syllables said something in Spanish, something
in English, something about sterility, something about tubes.

I am plump and soft and have not always had this hair—
always damaged. Always ruined, sent away to be fixed

and corrected. I am America's opaque shadow, tossed
like a dog rotting on every country roadside.

I've been HeLa cells passed around like Halloween candy.
Are the doctors still waiting

for their black offering? Me, a silk dress of skin?
Consider this:

each moment I am perched on an examination table
is my break, diseased heart, taken child.

This is how I feel: wide. Dark. Lumpy. Cotton
at the bottom of a pillowcase. My cartilage

has been trustworthy in its role,
how it performs its designed duty,

how it keeps fastened my flesh
to my bone. If I could be more

than a specimen, more than a collection
of daffodils, *flora* would mean I was not here.

Don't you see? I am still here on all fours.
I was never bone, nor beast, nor symbol for suffering.

I am a compass for warnings, a cured tissue.
They are still dressing me for the cut

and I prep for the familiar
cold gauze turned warm, then wet, then red.

Eulogy for Jamal

Do not imagine the black
burnt shotgun wound
tunneling my neck, or the shells

on the truck's floor. When a counter
sits between me and a gun dealer,
the pills have stopped muffling

crude cut voices. Your voice—
that numbing sound. Don't try to calm me.
Mother, don't press your couched hand

to my shoulder or *coo coo* slight syllables.
My throat, an opened
wailing, an overturned hive

rakes against my jaws.
When you bury me
and that velvet sound is finally flung

far away, imagine your lawn,
imagine the trim bushes, your bird feeder
—not me, or my arms strung

like loose vines in my lap.

Women of Purple Days
after Alice Walker

1. Disassociation

*"Although the widow's body
recovered, her mind was never the
same. She continued to fix her
husband's plate at mealtimes..."*
—*The Color Purple*

Butter beans, steamed corn, maybe field pea soup. *I don't even want to say nothing.* **Dear, is that you?** Who understands why a man will pull another man out of his house? **No.** Who can stand in an empty field and wait for someone to turn them loose? **Fish, barbecue pigtails, candied carrots.** Who understands why a rope is enough? **Pecan pie, dumplings, neck bone stew.** *Every time I open my mouth nothing come out but a little burp.* **Is that you at the door?** I seen what they do. I seen how they bring back a body charred or bloated. **Did they bring you back?** Better they throw me off a cliff. **What will you eat tomorrow?** *I don't fight. I stay where I am told. But I am alive.* **Collards, kale, spinach.**

Everything your pa touch, blossom. I dug my hands down in the dirt, gave them half the seed and I'm still afraid they won't let me make it home. *I don't know what she think about, but I think about angels.* **Rabbit stew, gizzards and rice.** So why would I undo the rope. *It so quiet you can hear the embers dying back in the stove.* **Go to sleep. You'll see your pa in the morning.** *Sound like they falling in on each other.* Ain't nothing outside of Georgia now. All I got is a hand that senses the change in weather. **You let your dinner get cold again. Are you home, dear?** *I make myself wood.* **No.** It tells me to hold tight, let the hot breeze roll by. **I can wait up. I can get started on tomorrow's cake.** *A tree.*

2. Squeak's Bop

I was never anyone's wild beast,
straddle-legged stance, puffing all my lungs' air
through my nose. How did I end up
in a man's juke joint sipping his hooch
and fighting off his wife? I was supposed to be
a prize. A throne bird.

I've been your slave, Ever since I've been your faith.

Harpo liked to stroke his finger on the pale side
of my arm, said he would never
have me under field sun, said after his first wife,
I was the neck he wanted to lean into
the curl of baby hair that tickled his burnt spine.
Who knew I was his just for now? Who knew
my winter bed was stand in?
Never said he'd send me for her.

But before I be your dog, I'll see you in your grave.

Sofia watched. Nerve broken stare, cell bound black,
she saw me pushed into the corner, and was pleased.
Like my bare buttocks was proof I was not a new wife.
She never muttered a word. The wardens sweat
dripped on my back and when he was done.
She hunkered back to her mat on the floor.

3. Ode to Sofia's Mouth

mouth of racket and cry   you
broken mouth   you   tattered
child   untwisted   lip
upturned silence   who told
this   mouth   to   speak?
damned teeth crooked chin
wild open jaw
taut cheeks   tongue-tied   locked
and loud   exasperated bark   sickly
cough   she stay silent and what
you get for it?   let the mouth
do   what it came to do
mouth of needing   mouth of want
speaking mouth   ~~un~~censored

        mouth

made   of dull wooden stump
the lowest piano key   stifled
sound mouth full   of swollen fists
what are your risks?   what music
you made   when they cut
your vocal chords   Sofia
keep leaning   into the girl
     of yourself
oh   Sofia   keep laughing

4. MR. _____'s Blues

> "...fact is, you got to give 'em something.
> Either your money, your land, your
> woman or your ass."
> —Mr._____

Wife, your man with small hands
has no excuses. When I wake,
my mouth tastes smoke. Do you understand

how their stares can be intent on breaking?
How someone's bent knee
yearns to thrash against my throat?

They dream of weight and hoof
squeezing out my inhale.
Here, a man might bleed you for dinner.

I have seen how they take
from manure-colored men with too much
honesty and a full safe,

make them twist and plead.
Yesterday, they let me go
only to become a stumbling chicken tomorrow.

I am another pesky mouse
in their garden. Each night I lay
in my uncomfortable sleep. In my dreams

the world cocoons itself into cotton
and tries to suffocate me.
Am I the rot of the world? A threat? A traitor?

When they are done with our neighbors,
they will pass me the shovel.
They will tell me to dig.

American Family: A Syndrome
Blood Washer's Syndrome

Blood   Blood   Blood
There is   so much blood on the
walk   Blood

        Blood
Blood   Blood There is
so much blood on the walk   Blood
Blood   Blood
    Blood There is   so much
blood on the walk
       Blood

       Blood
       Blood
       Blood

    There   is

so   much   blood
   on   the

      walk Blood

BloodBloodBloodThereissomuch
blood *BloodBlood There is somuch blood on the walk* od
Thereissomuchbloodonthewalkisblood
BloodBloodBlood Thereissomuchbloodont
hewalkBloodBloodBloodThereissomuch
blood on the walk
  Blood There is so much blood on the walk
Blood
Blood   Blood   Blood   There
is   so much blood on the walk Blood

Temporary Disorder—
Triggered by repeated viewings of video-recorded police killings, often in a single day, a Blood Washer patient, typically a father, develops an inexplicable urge to wash sidewalks. In the early stages of this illness patients spend prolonged moments looking at the floor or their feet. Though early symptoms of the Blood Washer's Syndrome surface in various ways, the disease fully initializes when the patient, in a hypnotic-like trance, wanders outside carrying a bucket. His movements become methodical. He will start on any street corner, rinse an area of pavement, apply detergent, rinse the section then continue to the adjacent area and repeat the sequence. During this lapse patients do not pause for food, water, or bathroom breaks. Not to be confused with Coffin Maker's Syndrome, Blood Washers intermittently repeat "Blood. Blood. Blood. There is so much Blood on the walk."

Symptoms can exhibit for hours or days. Often times, once the trance lifts subjects are unaware that they have been under the Blood Washer's trance. Many feel disoriented and nausea when the trance breaks.

If early signs of the Blood Washer's Syndrome are exhibited in a possible patient's behavior it is best to avoid late night television, YouTube, Facebook, and Twitter for two weeks. Ultimately it is best for the patient to submit himself to psychological observation for 48 hours or until early symptoms subside.

Car Slams into House, Lands on Sleeping Man

Imagine the collision: broken windows; the dozed
head, suddenly jolted; his picture frames tumbling
off egg colored walls, tangling with feet and linen; the driver,
all torso and legs twisted into the dash; a smashed
TV; wrecked walls' blooming insulation pink; the shock
of an engine's motor; the whistle and hiss under mangled hood.
Imagine the squeeze and press of a machine.
Once, my mother's muscles lapsed
and a paralysis jumped her left toe, drove up her body,
and pinned her to her bedroom floor. She says she fell
into a dream, that she was swimming in the river, that the heaviness
was the kick and strain of legs against water. Imagine awakening
to the shattering crash of dead weight, legs pressed in place.
I imagine the man, calm in soft layers of sheets, dreamed
of elephants, that he was tramping through a jungle,
that the elephants trumpeted a laugh when he used his arms
to imitate the hook and sway of their trunks. Not a second
to consider flat tires, a motors' tick, another's dinted trunk
popped open and bobbing. Not startled, not at all alarmed.

Your Eyes Have Never Looked This Stunning

You finally get gray eyes
when you go blind,

when everyone is a blurred
cloud with arms hugging

and grabbing, when someone
has to describe in whispers

the silver satin wrapping paper
and shiny ribbons of your Christmas gifts,

when the hand of your dying brother
resting on his bed

is indistinguishable from a hat.
You face familiar voices, nod

at all the fluttering sounds.
Behind the cornea, remember

your lemon colored furniture
the mouth of your favorite glass.

Remember those mud brown eyes
stared back from your mirror.

Remember how you hated
your dirty dishwater pupils

and dull mule skin. Remember
each morning you wished

for one pretty thing to look at.
Your eyes have never looked this stunning—

never have your gray eyes looked.

Chicken

I find my husband at our kitchen sink,
wrist-deep in the chest of our daughter's
chicken. Nearby, she sticks a pale finger

into a bloody clump of feathers on the counter.
He's wrung the bird's neck all wrong.
The head hangs by mangled threads of skin,

and shakes every time he rams his hand
down its cavity. I shove him aside.
Using my fingers I enter the bird, grip

and pull everything out into the hot air.
When I grab the heart, a bone snaps, but
it's got to come out. Our daughter watches me

rinse its chest and push its neck skin back
towards the body. He is still behind me.
I consider sending her to her room, instead,

I put her to slicing carrots. A girl must learn
proper gutting, how to take a chicken,
and run a blade clean through its throat.

Ostrich Woman

When I said I could not see her
ostrich legs, stock-still and raw-boned
under her blanket, her grayed tangled hair,

her chapped lips, the gummy sleep
smeared in the corner of her eyes,
nor hear urine running out of her,

nor the clatter of dusty shuttered blinds,
nor millet worms twisting
through the flour, no dented cans

dribbling soup or creamed corn
on her kitchen floor, no misplaced diaper,
no burnt cornmeal grains floating in black oil,

how rotted stairs to my childhood
bedroom sagged, how each door creaked
and hung through their open and slam, the letters

about aid and care and rejection of pay,
so much mail, so many envelopes,
the piles of things in the dim living room

in front of her stained love seat,
the cheap extension cords running
from the neighbor's fence,
a soiled bathroom and buckets, a crippled wing

I mean a crippled wheel chair
I mean my mother, her voice
I mean her walking, her dancing.

Why I Don't Call On Cops

If my brother locks himself into a bathroom
    and thinks his body has shattered
        into a constellation of broken light,

if for three hours I plead
    for him to unlatch
        the door, to let me in

even if his brain refuses to get ahold of itself,
        I do not call.

Though his thoughts are lost in the slim slant of night
    and his head over-swamped in lead,
        though he takes off again,

running through the living room,
    turning over kitchen spoons
        and threatens me with a potato peeler, I do not call.

How can I trust they won't treat him like a corpse?

I have watched the ballet of brutality
    break the bodies of strangers.
        I have seen the limp drag of a bird's bulleted wing.

A mind set to pasture will chew on its own blood source.

I am pleading with my brother:

They will not love you.

Or I am yelling as high as my lungs can yell:

I will not call.

Or I am only trying to say
    when my head takes its risks, let it bloom,
        let it devour its dead limbs.

Notes

"Anarcha Appears Again And Again" was inspired by Rachel Eliza Griffiths photography especially *Excerpt from 'Mule & Pear' Series, Mississippi 2014*

"Women of Purple Days":
    —"Disassociation": All of the italicized words are direct quotes from the novel, *The Color Purple*

    —Squeak's Bop": The italicized words are borrowed lyrics from Billie Holiday's song, "Billie's Blues"

Additional Acknowledgments

I wish to express gratitude to my colleagues, family, and friends whose support made this collection possible including Terry Blackhawk, Shashu Harris, Sydney James, Una Lee, Harlan Mack, Toni Moceri, Sophia Softky, Ryan Walsh, Ross White and all of the Grinders, and Daniel Wisner. Thank you to my families, the Comers, the Sanders, the Samuels and the McAfees. I love you.

Many thanks to the organizations and writing groups that supported the development of this work including Black Poets Speak Out, Allied Media Projects, Cave Canem, the African American and African Diaspora Studies Department at Indian University, the Indiana University Creative Writing Program, InsideOut Literary Arts Project, and Vermont Studio Center.

Thank you Ross Gay, Perry Janes, Ife-Chudeni Oputa, and Devin Samuels for your keen eyes. This work does not exist without your work.

Every word I write is in concert with writers who continue to astonish me with their work, scholarship and support: Tommye Blount, Kahn Davison, Vievee Francis, Aricka Foreman, francine j. harris, Airea D. Matthews, Jamaal May, Matthew Olzmann, and Scheherazade Washington Parrish.

Always and forever, thank you to Detroit.

Thank you Denis Rochac, Saeed Mulagata and Menelik Sanders I am forever grateful for your patience and support.

To mama and dad, may you rest in peace.
America, this book is for you.

N<small>ANDI</small> <small>COMER</small> received a joint MFA/MA in Poetry and African American and African Diaspora Studies at Indiana University. She has received fellowships from the Callaloo Creative Writing Workshop, Cave Canem, Vermont Studio Center, and Virginia Center for the Arts. Her poems have appeared in *Detroit Anthology* (Rust Belt Chic Press, 2014), *Blue Shift Journal, Crab Orchard Review, Green Mountains Review, Pluck!, Prairie Schooner,* and *Southern Indiana Review.* She is the author of the forthcoming collection, *Tapping Out* (Northwestern University Press).

CPSIA information can be obtained
at www.ICGtesting.com
Printed in the USA
LVHW02s0035300818
588620LV00004B/63/P